Good Food

I Like Chocolate

By Robin Pickering

Welcome Books

Children's Press
A Division of Grolier Publishing
New York / London / Hong Kong / Sydney
Danbury, Connecticut

Photo Credits: Cover, pp. 5, 7, 9, 11, 13, 15, 17, 19 by Jeffrey Foxx; p. 21 © Comstock, Inc.
Contributing Editor: Jennifer Ceaser
Book Design: Michael DeLisio

Visit Children's Press on the Internet at:
http://publishing.grolier.com

Cataloging-in-Publication Data

Pickering, Robin
    I like chocolate / by Robin Pickering.
      p. cm—(Good food)
    Includes bibliographical references and index.
    Summary: This book presents ways of enjoying chocolate, from drinking hot chocolate to
baking chocolate-chip cookies.
    ISBN 0-516-23083-2 (lib. bdg.)—ISBN 0-516-23008-5 (pbk.)
    1. Confectionery—Juvenile literature   2.   Chocolate—
Juvenile literature   [1.   Confectionery   2.   Chocolate]
I. Title   II. Series
TX783+ 2000
641.3'374—dc21
                                              00-20921

Contents

Do you like chocolate?

I like chocolate!

5

I like chocolate when it is hot.

I like to drink hot chocolate.

I like chocolate when it is cold.

I like to eat chocolate ice cream.

9

Sometimes I eat hot and cold chocolate together!

I like chocolate ice cream with hot chocolate **sauce**.

11

I like chocolate when it is soft.

My sister and I eat chocolate **pudding** at lunchtime.

13

I like chocolate when it is hard.

I eat a lot of chocolate candy on Halloween!

I like little bits of chocolate. These are **chocolate chips**.

My mom and I like to make chocolate-chip cookies.

I like chocolate in **mole** (**mo**-lay) sauce.

It is made with chocolate, **nuts**, **peppers**, and **spices**.

How do you like to eat chocolate?

20

21

New Words

chocolate chips (**chok**-lit **chipz**) small
   pieces of chocolate

mole (**mo**-lay) chocolate-flavored sauce

nuts (**nutz**) dry seeds with hard shells

peppers (**pep**-erz) a red fruit with a hot
   taste

pudding (**pud**-ing) a soft food that is sweet

sauce (**saws**) something poured over food

spices (**spys**-ez) dried plants and seeds

To Find Out More

Books

Chocolate (What's for Lunch)
by Claire Llewellyn
Children's Press

Kids' First Cookbook
by the American Cancer Society
American Cancer Society

Web Site
Hershey's Kidztown
http://www.hersheys.com/kidztown/index.html
Take a tour of a chocolate factory. Play some chocolate games.
Shows you foods you can make using chocolate.

Index

About the Author
Robin Pickering is a writer, editor, and yoga instructor living in Brooklyn, NY.

Reading Consultants
Kris Flynn, Coordinator, Small School District Literacy, The San Diego County Office of Education

Shelly Forys, Certified Reading Recovery Specialist, W.J. Sahnow Elementary School, Waterloo, IL

Peggy McNamara, Professor, Bank Street College of Education, Reading and Literacy Program